Clayre Benzadón

Liminal Zenith

SurVision Books

First published in 2020 by
SurVision Books
Dublin, Ireland
Reggio di Calabria, Italy
www.survisionmagazine.com

Copyright © Clayre Benzadón, 2020

Cover image © Nusya Krasovitskaya, 2020

Design © SurVision Books, 2020

ISBN: 978-1-912963-11-9

This book is in copyright. No part of this publication may be reproduced, stored in a retrieval system, or transmitted in any form or by any means without the prior permission in writing from the publisher.

Acknowledgments

Grateful acknowledgment is made to the editors of the following, in which some of these poems, or versions of them, originally appeared, or are about to appear:

The Acentos Review: "Horchata Moonshine" and "The Raw Yes"
Closet Cases anthology (Et Alia Press, forthcoming in April 2020): "Dapper"
Laurel Moon: "Horchata Moonshine" (an earlier draft)
Poetry Breakfast: "Sunflower Song" and "Zenith"
QA Poetry: "Lunacy"
SurVision: "Ephemera", "Pink Moon", and "Wheatfield Treehouse"

This Work is Dedicated to...

Liz Bradfield—this chapbook would not have been possible without your constant guidance and support my advisor and wonderful teacher! To Dawn Skorczewski, my mentor and professor who has helped me turn the tough and raw into beautiful pieces of writing. To Kirun Kapur. To Professor Quinney. To Professor Rebecca Morgan Frank, loving, humble educator who believed in me and gave me the confidence and courage to bring my dream closer to reality through the MFA application process. To Maureen Seaton, a very important advisor and friend to me, forever full of love and support. To Jaswinder Bolina, my thesis advisor, for providing me with such precise feedback and guidance. For Holly Iglesias, for helping me to access a part of my family history and myself through the introduction of documentary poetics. To Mia Leonin, for supporting me through the struggles of teaching. To Evelina Galang, a powerhouse of warmth and generosity. To Chantel Acevedo, our director, for the continued encouragement, for listening. To my friends, especially those from the University of Miami MFA cohort, who have been with me through the best, through the falls, for giving me the strength to write these poems, especially the more challenging subjects, and to my honors project group, for the intimate trust and support we have lent each other.

To my family, for their endless and continuous love and support for everything they have done to bring me to the place where I am right now, and for giving me the opportunity to receive such an important education.

To Tyler (and Thaly, my kindred spirit)—for everything—I love you.

Contents

LUNACY	6
April's Armlock	7
Lunacy	8
Horchata Moonshine	10
Ephemera	12
DECLINATION	14
Autumn Salad	15
Wheatfield Treehouse	16
Dando una Torta	18
DESIRE	20
Dapper	21
Desire	22
The Raw Yes	24
Sunflower Song	26
Unwinged	27
LIMINAL	28
Nocturna	29
Liminal	30
Pink Moon	32
The Color of Gravity	34
ZENITH	35
Self-Existing Omen	36
How to Feed the Wind	38
Zenith	39

Lunacy

Acrid hallucinations will smile at you, a waning insanity slivered links connecting the moon's phases together.

"A doctor once told me I feel too much. I said, so does god. That's why you can see the Grand Canyon from the moon."

—Andrea Gibson

April's Armlock

Tip of the days start in April,
in *lip, rip, rap,* deadened under
aperture of *aperire*,

initiation of openings, sweet pea slashings—
necked daises rising as Aries might,
slip of speech, of air, lapped under pails, paired
impulses craving in sun-soaked ice
drift transformed into sand meadows eclipsed—
now I am the ram, headed

towards anything to bang into, because hard-
headed, the skull doesn't break as bad as thoughts,
bang and *bang,* says *keep your mind until*

hurt leaves and you're restless, jasmine
crushed under season of the unsettled
nerves— crumbles under busted lamb frame
bucking April, reminding me of my horns, unfurled.

Lunacy

Women, ward off delirium
by tying a skull around your belt.

Then remember to place the lunacy
in your hands. Under the gums.

Acrid hallucinations will smile at you,
the braincase a protection against Styx.

Phoebe, shining Titan, fell just
like that without it, from Nyx.

Night is a frantic cavity
where warriors marked star

god Coyolxāuhqui mad, cut
off her limbs, tossed her head

into the heavens so that she could
become full again, her face a crescent

painted with bells, and eagles
flying down her hair.

Claws scraped her scalp bare
until her head tore open, her

cranium crowned.
Mother Coatlicue consumed

herself watching this, died from
insatiable insanity.

After, her belly miraculously fell
with a blessing, hummingbird

feathers balled up, violently
jammed, born into her chest,

the same way
month-sickness

collects into umbral
bales, filled with lune,
convex diurnality,
moon sick with the missed

cycle of Venus' own
hormonal rhythm.

Women, it is not enough
to wish, to crack with demand.

Instead, surrender. Pray to reach
a blue god, maybe Vishnu.

Then settle, with the atmosphere
melting away in fantastic ablation.

Horchata Moonshine

spills into the village of
La Aldehuela, a silver
river of whitewashed
buildings below the milk-
drunk Ávila galaxy:
La Via Láctea.

My dad points to the stars,
outlines them with chalky
atmosphere: *Captura todo
lo que reluce.* Capture

everything that glistens:
celestial incandescence,
earthshine of the wet moon,
lunar ray's refraction all

melted against my glass of horchata.

Yesterday, I held the cup up towards
the indigo flames of the Queimada
nebula and chanted along with the
alcoholic blaze burning witchcraft:

Fuerzas de aire, tierra, mar y fuego:
I am a spark of constellation bottled
up in a glass flask of fireflies.

Levantaré las llamas
de este infierno
como fuego:

I'll raise the hell-ridden
flames of this fire
 and combust.

Ephemera

In one day, a mare
rams into a hare, seizes
it, pares skin with her teeth.

She bows into dimness,
peers into hampered eventide
to find ephemeron: mayfly, double
adult and life-
cycle flyfished

with bucktail, handled
by a figures' back cast,
tip of the rod upwards,
leaving surface dark

on a young blue giant,
bluefish turned into rare star.

Harm burns there, above,
in the blueshifted sky,

where polar rabbits'
tracks are blueprinted,
tied with a blood knot.

There, the atmosphere
shifts through multiple
stages of development,

instars, nymphal
form fossilized,
like the insect

hatched into
plasmatic matter,
until it passes,
charging through,

attaining imago.

Declination

There is always a sufferable rim that will feed grip with drift, decline, swerve.

The sink into deviation marks the point on the heavenly celestial sphere imagined in the moment of stupor, when the vertical angle of danger breaks loose, exposure on thin ice.

Autumn Salad

Bask in melon nectar
of today's squelch,
tangelo sweat.

Sit next to the persimmon
tree, sip ripe salmon
stream, current

breaking open
fish, rippled scales,

severed marigolds, a flame field.
You'll want to share it,
apricot-small part of this trip,

near the little cottage,
drink up tea the heat brings,

cut up carrots, tomatoes,
autumn salad split with
orange safety, pumpkin

    sunset,

       sheltered
    dusk.

Wheatfield Treehouse

Wheatfield for miles.
White heat feeds the weeds durably.
The feet that land on the stalks
lead onto the marsh, eat the malt

and the leftovers, held
in between toes, wielding
spikelets like claws.

There is only you
in the grain maze.
Stalk heads split
sideways, hold

themselves like electric
slits. After silence
comes terror.

A life fit for lightning people.
Buckets fill with bearded
cartwheels.

The only lane of desert
is pollen, umber,
teddy bear treehouse,

an antique
lace rarity,

bolt of soft
red winter.

Dando una Torta

Sizzled *shhs*
on the pan after
loud patting of hands

kneading masa, tortillas
slapped as if they were

the small pat of las
sandalias right below
my seven-year-old ankles.

It looks so easy, the way Margarita
dips her hands in water, Miami
sunlight glinting

on her wrists while she smooths
out moisture—*es así*—folding
it again into a perfect oval,

  flattened reminder
  of something sweeter.

    quiero pancakes,

I say. Mi querida segunda madre,
paid to mother me, stares hard,
furrowed—

Sin vergüenza.

Her mouth curls around
the sour word, bland dough
of her work, soggy,

and now I see the bubbling
privilege, syrup, batter,
light ease, what it smothers—

younger, I replaced the laborious
shape with complacency,

abandoned her intimate faith,
her palms pounding cornmeal
until it calloused her hands,
the warmth in her work
unteachable, her native

Salvadorean hammered
    into flap-
      jacks—

with her culture jack-
hammered, floppily
integrated into
the griddled mix,

now, yes, only now
do I see desapercibido.

Desire

From Latin *desiderare*: "await what the stars will bring," from the phrase *de sidere*, "from the stars".

Things depart from us when we want them most, the strong feeling, the base, open-mouthed, unconscious unrestraint.

Dapper

I sit alone
in my room, observe
my slanted, framed self
displayed in a dress.

My arms glint awkward
beneath thin
straps of black satin,

skirted fabric pressing
knees, flabby at the waist.

See, I prefer a certain type
of tenderness, a vested mid-

riff loose-fit uncovering,
the kind where I openly

settle down in baggy pants,
roll up my sleeves,

all accentuation of muscle,
collar, adjusted with a neck-
tie, balancing out unrestrained

hang of a suit—how it stands
so easy this way, lets my
body become unbound.

Desire

Am I restless
for you

or because
of you?

In bed, I ache,
we both do,
from the stars'

fractures, their lucent
caresses palpable

without our hold,
beyond us, yet so

close to dying on hung
pane, its frame jamming

glare and hum of another
night without sleep.

I watch your face in
mystic slumber, touch

your cheek, then examine
fatigued eyes
beginning to open.

I catch
your grasp

before it leaves again
into that unconscious
trance.

Things depart from us
when we want them most.

I inhale warmth
and longing, fluid

and sensitive when
you almost awake again,

my gaze intense,
flitting between
your shot slits,

my want live,
dire, before you
are gone again.

The Raw Yes
(inspired by Anne Sexton)

Tell me what
the correct yes
means:

silk of skin
slipping through my
tongue, wrung with
fuck as you suck me,
  wholly fed,

 me singing
for my bedded thirst,
taste of a shared,

swallowed utterance,
lengua-
   je gemido,

my dare to live

as a woman of many
hearts, a big-noised
cicada call, wing-ticks

dripping honey-
dew notes.

I never not want.

Soy la maga de tus sueños,
deseo comer, more, *come*
here, delightful refreshment,

pura, dura, let me eat you
　　raw, entirely.

Sunflower Song

Bleeding heart, bloodroot.
The boneset of calla shuts

up the body of windflower
chimes, bluebells ringing

inside ghosted globe
thistles, darting

golden buttons. Yellow
archangels trumpet

the mouths of tulips
until they become a sun-

flower, summer
savory, heliotropism,

the way they face day-
light, a sweet asylum

in the symmetrical
stretch toward its golden
       angle.

Unwinged

After Lee Ann Roripaugh's "Underworlded"

You undo me each time. Your
body bends, convulses into a thumbtacked
throbbing, a quivered syntax, you heart
under your breath. It's honey lozenge, unwinged
longing fluttering with suffering, worm
-tickled warmth pecks combed into twisting
orange peels, hand-blossomed torch lilies on
xeriscape, bow-gripped torso breaking under the
biting lilium lip—the tips devour fresh silver
light, fracture window's first morning-pin's
clasp on nectar's light, burn a luscious rotisserie.

Liminal

A continuum at the edge of structure, fragmented between luminal and millennial, neither here nor there. Liminality is frequently likened to death, to being in the womb, to invisibility, to darkness, to bisexuality, to the wilderness, and to an eclipse of the sun or moon. It suspends like gravitational force, pulls understanding at the threshold of transformation, simultaneously hollow yet full, novel yet mundane in cultural space, a mystic revolution.

(part of excerpt taken from Victor Turner's "Liminality and Communitas")

Nocturna

There is no rest when you shiver night's seams.
You can climb out the frame of your window
and drown out cricket-whispers, clicked tight beam

high enough to jump from. You can look down,
watch the pulsing moon anguish in limbo,
impossible when it seeps hours, sheds crown-

ed wax of jaguar inked in the smudged sky.
You land. The shrubs blink while you tiptoe.
    Dangle in silence. Let it keep you nigh.

Liminal

Liminal space
is mineral limbo
grinding in

the mill of
threshold.

A continuum at the edge
of fragmented still

between
luminal and millennial.

Seizure
youth.

Between it,
ween off the teen
betting on lone

scope of surreal
possibility while

growing antlers
out of your mouth,

bite on the rim of
a watermelon's
rinds until they

stick out,
ridiculous,

limining a lime-
light

where a lone
thumbtack

should have
    gone.

Pink Moon

The moon walks.
It's a lamb-dancer,
bleats pink moss
and phlox,

always moves backwards
while walking forwards.

That's the thing:
any step ahead
means going back.

You spend time
painting a piñata,
then pinning it
to a pole, to get

a good hit,

then it swings
in reverse.

Peel it back,
the paper-mâché
ribbon and tinsel,

slit the cow
to let ashes
fall. Good luck

leaves that easily.
Essence of raisin,
wood fire, pine
cone,

keep the moon
moving. This coral
fish egg

tinges pink
with early
beastings.

The Color of Gravity

    Does it feel good, to lay your head
like that underneath the wrong.
    Yes, we are actually afraid of that
suspended thaw.
    Is it the gnaw of shore then, the lap
around a tired mouth, rubber, ajar.
    It's the tired wails of heat in the sand,
the sound of loose change deplete,
    weak acid rotting in the tooth,
head on fire while thinking.
    It's the week squeaking by, tense,
still depending on gravity to know best.

Zenith

*Under the world's spherical point, vernal tides bloom forth
seasonal resilience.
Zenith ties the location of the sky directly above an observer
with that of the most powerful locus, where both
heaven and observer become the highest
points crowned with celestial bodies, lighted and enlightened at
Zen's climax.*

Self-Existing Omen

Vandalized gravestones
tick x-marks-the-spot,

tick bomb threats,

crossed stickers,
swastikas

permanent on New York
subways. News

headline: *uptick of hate unclear.*

Of course, discrimination is always
ambiguous, in metro's speeding
tunnels, or in obscure

exoticism of my father's
face, stopped again
at airport security.

They'll check his luggage,
call the hardcover book
with foreign letters
religious extremism,

confiscate tefillin,
shema filled in

with a prayered shame,
eyes shut, aphonic

before the plane takes
off, before another smash,

before his amen
turns to omen.

How to Feed the Wind

You have to hold it out,
the wanting. Let it slap
in your palm, have the
flap unfold with a secret
skirting above conscious-
ness. Nest the head before
insomnia comes to pull it
down, whispers *there exists
no sort of senselessness.*
After, run, race the wind,
then win before it eats you.

Zenith

Above, the world
bursts eminence.

Mauve and mildew
residue lid lilacs,

corollas run off
on a split doze.

Under the spherical
point, vernal tides

bloom forth
seasonal resilience,

equinox and prime
seedtime, more growth.

Silence hints,
then fully coves

spring, singing
without me,

a single hymn ripped
out of the clouds.

More poetry published by SurVision Books

Noelle Kocot. *Humanity*
(New Poetics: USA)
ISBN 978-1-9995903-0-7

Ciaran O'Driscoll. *The Speaking Trees*
(New Poetics: Ireland)
ISBN 978-1-9995903-1-4

Helen Ivory. *Maps of the Abandoned City*
(New Poetics: England)
ISBN 978-1-912963-04-1

Elin O'Hara Slavick. *Cameramouth*
(New Poetics: USA)
ISBN 978-1-9995903-4-5

John W. Sexton. *Inverted Night*
(New Poetics: Ireland)
ISBN 978-1-912963-05-8

Afric McGlinchey. *Invisible Insane*
(New Poetics: Ireland)
ISBN 978-1-9995903-3-8

Anatoly Kudryavitsky. *Stowaway*
(New Poetics: Ireland)
ISBN 978-1-9995903-2-1

Tim Murphy. *The Cacti Do Not Move*
(New Poetics: Ireland)
ISBN 978-1-912963-07-2

Tony Kitt. *The Magic Phlute*
(New Poetics: Ireland)
ISBN 978-1-912963-08-9

George Kalamaras. *That Moment of Wept*
ISBN 978-1-9995903-7-6

Anton Yakovlev. *Chronos Dines Alone*
(Winner of James Tate Poetry Prize 2018)
ISBN 978-1-912963-01-0

Bob Lucky. *Conversation Starters in a Language No One Speaks*
(Winner of James Tate Poetry Prize 2018)
ISBN 978-1-912963-00-3

Christopher Prewitt. *Paradise Hammer*
(Winner of James Tate Poetry Prize 2018)
ISBN 978-1-9995903-9-0

Mikko Harvey & Jake Bauer. *Idaho Falls*
(Winner of James Tate Poetry Prize 2018)
ISBN 978-1-912963-02-7

Tony Bailie. *Mountain Under Heaven*
(Winner of James Tate Poetry Prize 2019)
ISBN 978-1-912963-09-6

Maria Grazia Calandrone. *Fossils*
Translated from Italian
(New Poetics: Italy)
ISBN 978-1-9995903-6-9

Sergey Biryukov. *Transformations*
Translated from Russian
(New Poetics: Russia)
ISBN 978-1-9995903-5-2

Alexander Korotko. *Irrazionalismo*
Translated from Russian
(New Poetics: Ukraine)
ISBN 978-1-912963-06-5

Anton G. Leitner. *Selected Poems 1981–2015*
Translated from German
ISBN 978-1-9995903-8-3

All our books are available to order via
http://survisionmagazine.com/books.htm